This
Read, Listen, & Wonder
book belongs to:

CANDLEWICK PRESS

Frogs are in danger — please help!

Rules for frog-lovers

◉ Don't ever take frog spawn from a pond in the wild.

◉ You should only take frog spawn from a man-made pond — and only take a LITTLE.

◉ Always take your frogs back to the pond they came from.

For Jane Slade
V. F.

For Rebecca, with much love
A. B.

Consultant: Martin Jenkins

Text copyright © 2000 by Vivian French
Illustrations copyright © 2000 by Alison Bartlett

First U.S. paperback edition with CD 2008

The Library of Congress has cataloged the hardcover edition as follows:

French, Vivian.
Growing frogs / Vivian French ; illustrated by Alison Bartlett. — 1st U.S. ed.
p.   cm.
Summary: A mother and child watch as tadpoles develop and grow into frogs.
ISBN 978-0-7636-0317-5
1. Frogs—Infancy—Juvenile literature. 2. Frogs—Growth—Juvenile literature. [1. Frogs.]
I. Bartlett, Alison, ill. II. Title
2L668.E2 F75   2000
597.8'9139—dc21   99-043695

ISBN 978-0-7636-2052-3 (paperback)
ISBN 978-0-7636-3831-3 (paperback with CD)

2 4 6 8 10 9 7 5 3 1

Printed in China

This book was typeset in Tapioca.
The illustrations were done in acrylic.

Candlewick Press
2067 Massachusetts Avenue
Cambridge, Massachusetts 02140

visit us at www.candlewick.com

Growing Frogs

Vivian French   illustrated by Alison Bartlett

CANDLEWICK PRESS
CAMBRIDGE, MASSACHUSETTS

Once, when I was little, my mom read me a story about a frog that grew **bigger** and **bigger** and **bigger**.

Afterward Mom asked me if I'd like
to watch some real frogs growing.

"I know where there's a pond with lots
of frogs' eggs in it," she said. "We could
bring some home."

I was frightened.
"I don't want any
frogs jumping around
getting **bigger**
         and **bigger**
                and **bigger**," I said.

But Mom gave me a hug. "It's only a story,"
she said. "Even when our frogs are grown up,
they'll still be smaller than my hand."

"Oh," I said. "Okay."

The next day we went to look at the pond. The water was dark brown, and there was gray jelly stuff floating on the top.

"Yuck!" I said.

"There's the frog spawn," said Mom.
And she pointed to the gray jelly stuff.
"I bet that was laid last Friday night.
The frogs were croaking so loudly,
I couldn't get to sleep."

Male frogs croak to attract female frogs for mating. Mating occurs when the male frog covers the female's eggs with his sperm. A tadpole will only grow if an egg joins with a sperm — this joining is called fertilization.

"You see the black dot in the
middle of each jelly shell?" said Mom.
"That's going to grow into a tadpole."

"Where are the frogs?" I asked.
"Tadpoles grow into frogs," she said.
"Little ones — no giant frogs here!"

Mom put some pond weed
and some stones into a bag.
She filled a bucket with pond
water. Then I scooped a
little of the frog spawn
into it.

Always use pond water for growing frogs at home.
Tap water has chemicals like fluoride in it
that might poison the frogs.

When we got home, we put everything into a big fish tank in the kitchen.

The cat kept peering at it, so we had to put a wire net over the top.

I counted
twenty-seven
little black dots.
Each dot was inside
its own jelly shell.

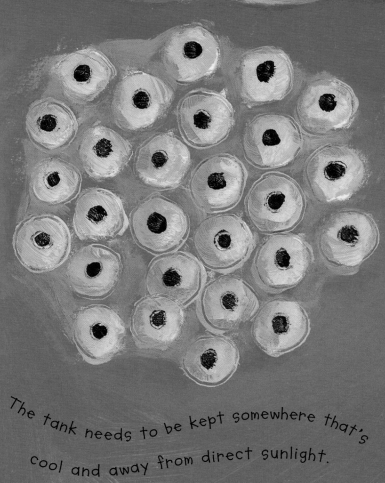

The tank needs to be kept somewhere that's cool and away from direct sunlight.

Every day when I woke up,
I went straight downstairs
to look at the frog spawn.

The little dots
grew into bigger dots,

and then into
tiny curls.

In a tank, the eggs hatch into tadpoles about ten days after they are laid.

And one morning
I saw the first tadpole
wriggling out of its
jelly shell!

At first the tadpoles didn't do much.
They just stayed close to their jelly shells
and nibbled at the pond weed.

But after two or three days
they looked quite different. There
were feathery things on their heads,
and I could see their eyes.

The feathery things are called gills, and they're
what underwater animals use for breathing.

They swam **very** fast.

Ten of the eggs
didn't ever hatch.
The black dots went
dull and cloudy,
and Mom took
them away.

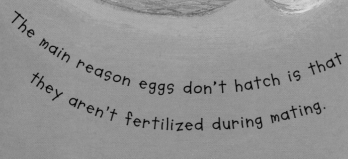

The main reason eggs don't hatch is that they aren't fertilized during mating.

Then we cleaned out
the tank and put in fresh pond
weed and pond water.
   One of the tadpoles swam
into my hand when I was
putting a stone back.
It was slippery and slithery,
and it made me jump.

After the tadpoles hatch,
the pond water needs
to be changed at least
twice a week.

After a while, I got used to having tadpoles, and I didn't look at them so often.

When Mom told me their little feathery things had disappeared, I didn't believe her.

But it was **true.**

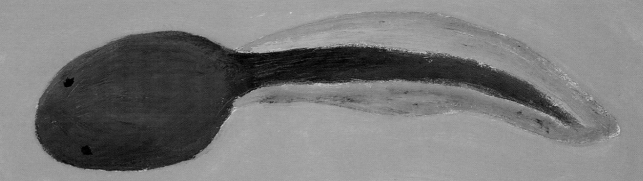

Tadpoles have gills on the outside of their bodies at first. Then they grow gills inside their bodies, and the outside ones disappear.

I was the one who saw the next change, though.

"Look!"

I shouted, and Mom rushed to see.

Some of the tadpoles had grown two little bumps. Mom said the bumps would grow into back legs.

They grew very quickly.

One day there were two little bumps.

The next day the bumps were stumps.

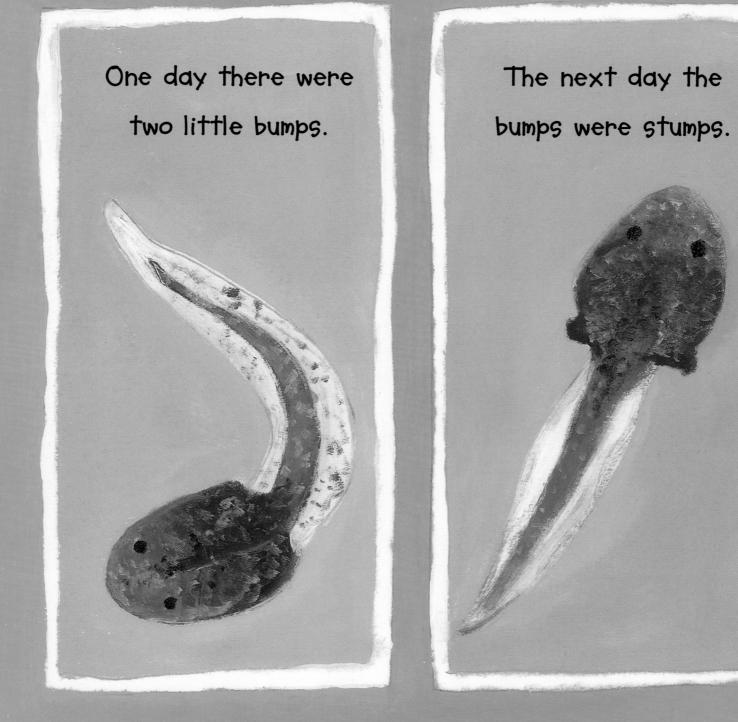

The day after that they looked like real legs.

And when the feet unfolded, they were webbed, like tiny brownish-green fans.

"They aren't tadpoles anymore," I said.
"They're not-quite-frogs."

The not-quite-frogs grew front legs next.

And then their tails got shorter . . .

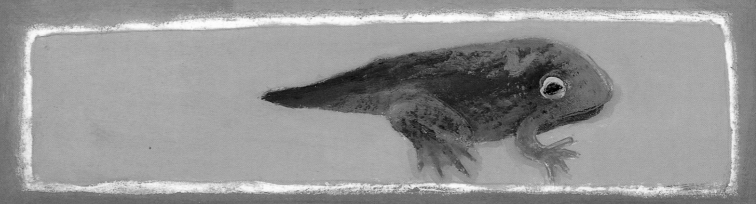

and their mouths got **w i d e r .**

"Now they're frogs," Mom said.

"Baby ones."

Soon the baby frogs were popping up and gulping at the surface of the water.

One of them tried to climb onto the stones, but it slid off. Mom said they were getting ready to leave the water.

"Grown-up frogs breathe air," she said. "That's what the stones are for — so our frogs can climb out of the water and breathe."

As tadpoles slowly turn into frogs, they grow lungs for breathing air, and their gills disappear.

Not long after that, Mom said it was
time to take our baby frogs back to live
in the pond with all the other baby frogs.

I was sorry to leave them, but Mom
said we could come back and visit
every day.

Baby frogs need space to grow and room to hop around.
Grown-up frogs live most of their lives on land,
returning to their ponds only to breed.

One rainy morning a week later

Mom woke me up very early.

"Hurry!" she said, and we ran downstairs

and out to the pond.

There were **hundreds** of tiny frogs hopping over the grass.

"They're looking for dark, wet places to live," Mom said. "But they won't go far, and in a couple of years they'll be back to lay frog spawn of their own."

"Will they be bigger then?" I asked.

"Just a little," said Mom.

"Good," I said. "I like having frogs jumping around getting **bigger** and **bigger** and **bigger!**"

29

Index

Look up the pages to find out about

all these froggy things.

Don't forget to look at both kinds of words —

this kind and *this kind.*

VIVIAN FRENCH has a lot of experience growing frogs. Every spring when her daughters were little, they visited the pond next door to collect frog spawn and watch the tadpoles hatch. She says, "My cat was always very interested."

ALISON BARTLETT says that before she started working on the illustrations for *Growing Frogs*, she thought frog spawn was "disgusting."
Now she thinks it's amazing!